THE INDOOR PARK

Sean O'Brien

THE INDOOR PARK

BLOODAXE BOOKS

ISBN: 0 906427 49 5

First published 1983 by
Bloodaxe Books Ltd,
P.O. Box 1SN,
Newcastle upon Tyne NE99 1SN.

Second impression 1993.

Bloodaxe Books Ltd acknowledges
the financial assistance of Northern Arts.

Cover printing by J. Thomson Colour Printers Ltd, Glasgow.

Printed in Great Britain by
Cromwell Press Ltd, Broughton Gifford, Melksham, Wiltshire.

Patrick O'Brien
1910-1981

Acknowledgements

Acknowledgements are due to the editors of the following publications in which some of these poems have appeared: *Aquarius*, *Encounter*, *The Honest Ulsterman*, *London Magazine*, *New Edinburgh Review*, *New Edinburgh Review Anthology* (Polygon Books, 1982), *The New Review*, *Poetry Review*, *Poetry Supplement* (Poetry Book Society, Christmas 1979), *Quarto*, *Stone Ferry Review*, *The Times Literary Supplement*, *To Build a Bridge* (Lincolnshire & Humberside Arts, 1982), and *White Room*. 'Air', 'The Real Barbarians' and 'Ryan and the Historical Imagination' were broadcast on *Poetry Now* (BBC Radio 3).

Fourteen poems selected from this collection also appear in Douglas Dunn's anthology *A Rumoured City: new poets from Hull* (Bloodaxe Books, 1982).

Some of these poems were included in a collection for which Sean O'Brien received an Eric Gregory Award in 1979.

Contents

9   The Snowfield
10   Walking
11   Air
12   Papers
13   Station Song
14   Le Départ
16   The Park by the Railway
17   Stories
18   Anne-Marie, the Flower Girl
19   At the Resort
20   The Real Barbarians
21   Victorians
22   The Disappointment
23   The Sun is Visiting the Sick
24   The Exiles
26   After Hours
27   The Police
28   The Name
29   The Brochure
30   Clio
32   Ryan and the Historical Imagination
33   William Ryan's Song in July
34   The Wild Ass Is Skint
35   In the Head
36   Jazz
37   For Lowell George
38   The Beat Goes On
40   The Next Meeting
41   Midsummer's Eve
42   Not Sending Cards this Year
43   The Widower
44   Downstairs
45   Infants
46   Those in Peril
48   The Seaside Specialist
49   Gun Law
50   Heatwave
51   Late
52   Quiet Wedding

53   The Ring
54   The Lamp
55   Tides
56   The Last Japanese Poet in the West
57   Bound for Glory
58   Victims
59   Sitting in the Draught
60   From the Narrator's Tale
62   Two Finger Exercise
63   The Captain's Pipe
64   The Amateur God

The Snowfield

It is so simple, being lonely.
It's there in the silence you make
To deny it, the silence you make
To accuse the unwary, the frankly alone.
In the silence you bring to a park
When you go there to walk in the snow
And you find in the planthouse,
Next to the orchids in winter slow-motion
And sleeping unreadable mosses,
Sick men, mad, half-born, who are sitting
As long as the afternoon takes.
Left there by helpers hours ago,
As if preparing for a test,
Each holds a book he cannot open.

Some days you put together
Sentences to say for them
As you leave to go back to the street.
With work they might be epigrams
Of love and modest government.
And this thought frees you. You pick up the paper.
You eat. Or you go to the library and talk.

But some days there is nothing
You cannot know. You still leave,
But it seems to take hours, labouring
Back to the street through the snowdrifts
And not worth the effort.
It seems that this is all there is.
It happens like snow in a park, seen clearly
After days of admiration, and looking
As if it had always been there, like a field
Full of silence, that is not beginning or ending.
It is so simple. You just hadn't looked.
And then you did, and couldn't look away.

Walking
(for Deborah)

I am in love with detail. Chestnut trees
Are fire-damaged candelabra.
Waterbirds are porcelain.
The planthouse is the room within the room
And all this is England,
Just left here, and what's to be done?

It does not remember the dances,
Silk stockings and murders and money.
We were not invited. We came late
To trespass on ourselves among the furniture,
Admiring the upholstery of Hell,
Where the talk is the best and you know it.

Adulterous cortège of cars around the park,
Where the couples are solving themselves with despair.
They will die of each other.
They have names, they were born –
If they're held to the light they have souls,
Like little ingots knocking at the heart.

O Vaughan and Geoffrey, Annabel and Jane,
Your time is up, you've gone professional.
You are condemned to live this script
Until the gestures make you retch,
And then forever, knowing it –
The passive yes, the nominated self,

The grammar till it vanishes,
Among these great facilities,
Where she and I are walking, I believe.
We're holding hands. I say, and then repeat,
There is no nightmare big enough to hurt,
Since it fits with the tick of the gold at my heart.

Air

I shall be writing you until I die,
You in your several selves, my friend of half a life,
My girl, my enemy, my judge.

An empire of affection built in air:
The air remains, the context of At Last.
It fills the space between the lives with words –

The last of everyone, through Caesar, Janis, Marx
And Ron McKernan, and from each
A democratic breath of silence

As helpful and useless as drink.
They died, and we diminished proteans
Have died as well, in every second thought.

We drew the map, and gave the place its names
Of water, light, and grass for lying on,
That single summer, standing at its heart.

—We didn't. We were not ourselves.
Nor are we now, when we've concluded
Every variant of hate.

We named each tic of sentiment, or not.
It's called *The Oxford Book of Early Life*,
And here's the long, uneasy supplement

That cannot trust its sources. Air,
And we can only add to it
Our passionate routine,

In case our scholarship should yield
The facts of how we lived and felt
And breathed the air behind the air.

Papers

You might go through my papers sometime,
Years from now but in weather like this,
An unexpected wind in June, the month
In which we met, that now accepts
No special pleas and simply shifts
Stacks to the floor, to the corners that hold
Love-letters and final demands.
Leave the window wide open and go.

You might hear from downstairs
The counterpane of what I wrote
Unmaking, remaking itself, still performing
The paperweight tricks of the master.
Let it light by chance
Upon what I cannot imagine now,
A natural disorder we could share.

Station Song

I should have seen you all the time, you ghosts,
But I was taken up elsewhere
With getting on, which got me here.
I'm back for good. You are
So patient, like the best of hosts.

Am I your guest?
The girl, is she one too?
You say there's nothing I must do,
That I am not accountable to you.
You wish me nothing but the best.

I try to see if I'll get lost.
I walk the streets. But then a sign
Propped up on bricks explains what's mine:
One door along this line
Of doors that open on to dust.

Le Départ

You've been leaving for years and now no-one's surprised
When you knock to come in from the weather.
The crew is past embarrassment:
They can live with their nautical names, and with yours.
So sit, take down your glass, and talk
Of all that is not you, that keeps you here
Among the sentimental stevedores
In the drinking clubs in the dank afternoons
Of your twenty-ninth year. There may be news.

Indeed. Somebody drowned last night, walked sideways
Off a Polish fishmeal hulk. A rabid Paraguayan bear
Was seen among the kindly hookers eating fruit.
A hand-carved coelacanth was found
When the cells were dug out to lay drains . . .

How can you not be struck by these arrivals?
The perfect boat is sailing Tuesday week.
It's heading southwards, way beyond the ice –
Starsailing seems quite plausible by night.
Until then there is querulous Ninepin
(The loss of his ticket for thieving)
And Madeleine's never-secret grief
(Be kind, and ask politely what)
And someone selling crocodiles
And hash from the sump of a jungle . . .
Now even the Juvaro have secret accounts –
Sell them your Service Forty-Five
And get a tape-recorder back . . .
The Amazon's an answering service:
No one's ever really lost. A month ago
Rocheteau, stuck for credit, offered up
The pelvic bones of Mungo Park
In exchange for a fifth of *Jim Beam*. . .
We always thought that Scot was lying about Africa.

It is easily night: soft boom of lighter-boats
Beyond the fogwall, swung on inauthentic tides
That left you here, that left you here
As the lovesongs go over the warehouse
Among patrolling cats and a lost A.R.P.
With his bucket of sand and his halberd.

You are doped on the stairs on the way to the moon
With Yvonne, who has aged but not quite,
Who knows the words to every song
And places one flattering palm on your spine
Till you move, who keeps a special bottle
For you (but half gone, half gone) by the bed,
A black fire of sugar that says all there is
About travelling. You're halfway there.

And all shall sing until the awful morning
Reminds them of themselves,
Then sleep in early restaurants,
Boastful of such daft endurance,
And then inspect the shipping lists
Until the time is right.

'You talk in your sleep,' says Yvonne.
'So I woke you. All this travelling –
You leave the girls for what?
Are we not always, always travelling?
Let's drink to that, and one before you go.'

The Park by the Railway

Where should we meet but in this shabby park
Where the railings are missing and the branches black?
Industrial pastoral, our circuit
Of grass under ash, long-standing water
And unimportant sunsets flaring up
Above the half-dismantled fair. Our place
Of in-betweens, abandoned viaducts
And modern flowers, dock and willowherb,
Lost mongrels, birdsong scratching at the soot
Of the last century. Where should we be
But here, my industrial girl? Where else
But this city beyond conservation?
I win you a ring at the rifle range
For the twentieth time, but you've chosen
A yellow, implausible fish in a bag
That you hold to one side when I kiss you.
Sitting in the waiting-room in darkness
Beside the empty cast-iron fireplace,
In the last of the heat the brick gives off,
Not quite convinced there will be no more trains,
At the end of a summer that never began
Till we lost it, we cannot believe
We are going. We speak, and we've gone.
You strike a match to show the china map
Of where the railways ran before us.
Coal and politics, invisible decades
Of rain, domestic love and failing mills
That ended in a war and then a war
Are fading into what we are: two young
Polite incapables, our tickets bought
Well in advance, who will not starve, or die
Of anything but choice. Who could not choose
To live this funeral, lost August left
To no one by the dead, the ghosts of us.

Stories

'You can, now that she's qualified.
Let nothing distract you,' he said.
We drank tea in the visiting hour
As if at our own kitchen table.
'Just go, the two of you.' As if we might
Transform your van into a house,
Add river, pasture, children
In one summer, forgetting ourselves
In the country he came from.

I thought he came from Nenagh.
No, he played football for them.
It's been Dublin, Cork and Limerick
And still he won't stop travelling.
'See, Cork is for strangers: it's short in the mouth
So it calls off the questions. But go.
A woman will console a man.'

Suppose we did. He'd never come.
A bad third novel in the sticks
With him wanting tea at all hours
And you delivering the dead.
He left the place. It's stories now
And they sustain no time, no life.
I've come so far from land I'd drown.

Anne-Marie, the Flower Girl

It could be true. There might just be
No outcome. After all the beds,

The halls with unusual prints,
The sculleries with mould that climbs

From teapots, all the headless birds
Left over by the cats, the years

Of unstoppable weather
You would think by now

She might have grown a bit suspicious.
So all the long-haired boys have gone

To India at last, but she
Keeps busy making things to sell.

The one she aways wanted lives
Across the street. She hardly hears

His annual excuse for still
Remaining with that other bitch.

The rooms get painted, cats renewed,
And this month's books are all begun.

A miracle is taking place.
So this is time, and time contains

Her history, and here she lives
Her history, from time to time.

At the Resort

In the pauses that follow the pauses
The ocean throbs back. All night it works
At the back of the hill that sits in his head.
From loyalty, he moves. He 'checks the window',
Peering for the little boat
Not used this summer, full of leaves
And water. It has rained a month.
He goes back, he does nothing at all.
But he hates the bright cups on the sniggering dresser,
The peat that wants laughter to feed it.

She has been doing things all night
To decorate contempt. She produces
Herself in that dress, with a cake
And hot whiskey, says, 'Read to me now.'
She knows about pastoral things.
The story of the man and girl
Who fight while travelling by car,
The one that first brought them to bed,
Whenever that was, whenever
His neck didn't ache and she wasn't knitting
Scarves with which to hang himself
In the trees at the foot of the garden,
Whenever the rain, or the hill, or the sea eases off.

The Real Barbarians
(for Susan McKay)

It is mid-afternoon
And the barbarians have been and gone.
How strange a scent is in the room
Without a girl to hold.
All day we have been staring out to sea
And fingering letters and·items of clothing
That hint a return that won't happen.

We do so because at the end of an age
You must live for such chances, such footnotes
As those that attracted them here,
Like grants, a spare room
Or the name of the place,
Which was strange to their ears
And remained so because they fucked off.

Now let us, sitting on these stools,
In a bar lit with rain, with a view of the harbour,
Give praise, in such voice as we have –
For our past has been thieved
By piratical girls from the West
With a mixture of sweetness, strong liquor and cunning
No provincial decadence could match.

Let's have no rage, plan no revenge,
Since history's our recompense:
Their novels, gleefully untrue,
Well show us lecherous and mad,
Brute sniggerers between epiphanies,
Half-pissed like this,
And what is worse, immortally.

Victorians

White heads, white hats, in garden chairs,
Enthusiasts of time,
Adulterous and hopeful men, who met
Their fallen girls at stations out of town:

This day of summer's yours in perpetuity.
I cannot love your manners or your work,
But accidental bravery persists,
In homiletic lilac and your vanity in stone.

We were the epic exegetes
And called religiose.
We are what's left when time retreats,
The syphilitic rose:

How honesty becomes opaque,
The season drawing on:
We looked into the little lake
And wanted to be gone.

Let this be noon, before the letter comes,
The daughter coughs, the verses are exposed,
Before the century goes black,
And you go blind, and all the doors are closed.

The Disappointment
(for Stuart Ross and John Pettenuzzo)

The sky becomes mother-of-pearl,
A lady's box of trinketry.
The air inside it can remember
Lavender at two removes,
Like someone's love once dreamed about
But not possessed, and longed for now.

In one of these burgherly houses,
Room on room on corridor,
It is someone's finale, unpacking herself
From lint and pins and looking-glasses.
Bland with young 'accomplishment'
Not even the letters are cryptic here,

Valuable only in histories of boredom:
Chat of some dud couple caught
In frames where time stands in for love,
With their backs to a sea to whose ironclad rightness,
Decked with pennants, fleet on fleet,
They bore unthinking witness. They were cold.

All afternoon I trudge around
Inventing tasks. I look and sniff
And find Victoria and Albert
Brilliant white and everpresent.
From windy plinths The Great outstare
The disappointment of their will

As dusk elaborates the park.
A duck-guffaw, a lacy hem of frost,
A salesman reading *Penthouse* in his car,
Pianoforte being taught and loathed –
Its sweet unwarranted effects,
Not brave enough for sorrow but still there.

The Sun is Visiting the Sick

The sun is visiting the sick
And laying its hands.
Who is there who could count
Its acts of charity with girls,
Upon the hands, the fingernails,
The eyes, the gold buckles of sandals
And the backs of knees
At bus-stops waiting to go
To Drumchapel or wherever
History is happening today?

We're always walking.
This is what we do
Before and after love.
Shall we ever exhaust the estate?
Who is there who can count
The rooms where we wake up?
With luck we shall open our eyes
And find someone to cough at.
Good morning, and have you a name?

Forgive me all the times I thought
Of sex and not the planned economy
With you or someone very like
In Govan in the Elderpark,
In Kelvinside, in Cambuslang,
Kincardineshire and Auchterarder.

The Exiles

The government in exile
Calls this city park its home.
These men have waited into age
For history to change its mind.
Survivors of an orchestra,
One night a week they play the tune
They always play, and hate the look
Of stale tuxedos wearing them
In the glass of the bookcase
Whose volumes dispose of their lives
By omission. Out on the park
The grass wears week-old snow
Like unchanged bandages, half-off.
The cold is offering its gloves
To the blue hands of walkers
Attempting the circular mile.
Black paths between black cherry trees
Are diplomatic avenues
And the avoidance of their friends
The residue of protocol.
The cadre in its overcoats
Goes coughing through the fog.
Each member pauses at a room
In which a woman tries to listen
To the phantoms of a café
In the square beside the river,
To the music of the homeland
That revolves upon the air.
Magniloquent, the frozen brass:
Its tongues are pure geography;
The spirit held behind the teeth
And swallowed into breathlessness
A distant fire to be borne,
Then loved again, like arts
Once sacrificed to principle
As students of a politik
Which changed their names and cast them out
Into this hired shadowplay.

It has always been too late.
Now the record will not change
Now the walkers circle, circle,
Drawn to the darkening centre.

After Hours

The drinks are left for dead. A pint of mild,
The colour of a smoker's lung, stares down
Into its black reflection, where old men
Are pickled, caught in toilets arguing.

A lemon at the bottom of its gin
Relaxes, squeezed and useless now, like girls
No longer young, who light up after sex
And swear, and think of putting on a face.

Strong lagers, chilling on cold shelves, predict
Collisions, bikers smashed like trays of glass,
Night pissing them away, at roundabouts
Where lights as yellow as their liquor watch.

The drinkers of unusual liqueurs
Shall go quite mad, the sherry-quaffers turn
The colour of old furniture, the wets
On lemonade get acid in the face.

The world is here as well, the residue
Of time got wrong, got lost, or not recalled,
Just looking at itself. It has no love
And will not change, and it is always shut.

The Police

No one believes them. Their windows get broken.
It rains in their yards and their kids
Dress in black and are sullen and pasty.
Their wives would like going to hangings:
They knit and they think about crime.

The police, they have allotments, too:
Like us they don't get paid.
But their beans are like stone
And their lettuce like kelp
And black men come on moonless nights
To burn the greenhouse down,
And their windows are broken
So they don't eat tomatoes.
The police, when they pot their begonias,
Press down with both thumbs, like that,
And a fly can be killed with one blow.

They are not jealous, the police.
When they stare at your allotment
They're sure there's a body below.
But if you say, 'Yes, he's a Roman,'
They ask you, 'And how do you know?'
We are all called *Sunshine*,
Or else we are liars, or both.
We would be better off without ourselves,
Or cordoned off, at least.
The world is guilty of itself,
Except the police, that is.

The police are not immortal, though they try.
They are buried with honours and bicycle clips.
But black men come from the allotments
And chop their gravestones down.
Then lots of queers with foreign names
Dig them up and make films of their bones.

The Name

Vlad the Impaler, the torturer's horse,
And the mercantile towers of Asia
Stacked with skulls like death's exchequer.
Something must be done with Sunday:
Florid libraries deputize for God.
When the light has run back through the page
I can hear the wind gathering leaves,
But one name in the cursory millions
Has lodged like a seed in my throat.
Katya, whom Anonymous has praised
Forgettably for being young and his
In summer thirteen twenty-six.
This is only a way of repeating her name,
A charm, that can't believe in time.
The wine my conscience drinks tonight
Can run as sweet and harsh as hers
Across my tongue. These apples cannot weigh
As firm and cool as hers upon my hands.

The Brochure

Built for bracing airs above the sea,
It shadows half the beach
And mines the sandstone cliff with larders.
Red brick, grey brick, yellow corners, square
And grosser than the national product.
Admire the glass-eyed Nemo-domes
And sawn-off fire-escapes
On the locked heights.
Behind the screams of hooded gulls
The screams of doomed remittance-men:
Behind them both, the rubber tread
Of floor-detectives, rigorously picked
From jails and noncommissioned ranks.
Their doctors' bags are pursed
For pliers, greaseproof packets,
The complete range of fillings,
Toenails and St Christophers,
Postal orders, things in lockets,
Oaths extracted on notepaper
Headed *The Grand*, plus the various
Snifters of morphine, the various
Samples of semen and blood.
Minute attention is their mark,
While lower down in sweating kitchens
Waiters redirect the pipes
To the bottling plant. At the cocktail hour
Fine goblets of urine appear
On silver trays on tables at the doors
Of virgin brides: beneath each glass,
Lubricious propositions, costed.
Following dinner, the dancing with swords
And the drawing of lots for the novelty gangplank,
Pickled parts are raffled, old songs sung.
Be assured that none is excluded.
In case there is an enemy
The highly trained homunculi
Who staff our deep torpedo rooms
Will fire you from sewer-pipes
Across the moonlit bay.

Clio
(for Dave Lewis)

Arcane and absolutist aunt
Refusing access over tea,
You are my private hierophant
And you embroider me.

You say you know me inside out,
This man I haven't met,
And you could tell me all about
What hasn't happened yet.

But nothing happens here at all
As far as I can see.
The missing pictures on the wall
Are how it's meant to be.

You have the leisure to be bored
And so you still trot out
The view that you must be adored,
Which I take leave to doubt:

Your ironies are second-rate,
Imagination nil –
So how do you concoct my fate,
And what about this will?

You smile that smile and preen yourself
And ply me with a bun:
You were the first one on the shelf
And all you've ever done

Is recognize my vanity,
And tease it till it screams,
Whilst feeling up my sanity,
The small coin of my dreams.

Gentility's as impolite
And secretive as cancer –
Both kick several shades of shite
From any life-enhancer.

Then I hear, 'Let's try again
And then you can go home.
It takes a little English pain
To build a metronome.'

So I'm reciting day and night
The masters and their grief.
I'll know when I have got it right
If boredom kills belief.

Remote and circular, your place
Evaluates my senses,
Palgrave's Golden Interface,
Dismantler of tenses,

Scholar-Critic's time machine,
Will Travel Anywhere,
Though somehow I have never been
Around when I was there.

So will you? Won't you? Should I care?
Has it ended or begun?
I do not know if I can bear
Interminable fun.

But I don't think I'll ever die.
I don't suppose you'll let me.
Every time I say goodbye
You threaten to forget me.

Ryan and the Historical Imagination

Coming to the end of it,
I prize my unilluminating life
For every tic of feeling, for its weather.

When she left, I remembered.
I only remembered. No one
Reproduces skin on skin
Or the thumbs on the hipbones.
Finally, she called us typical.
I took offence, and she took
Half the records and the books.
I prize this also, for having no name
But the one I began with.

We never photographed the streets
Before they tore them down.
The clearing she undressed in aged fifteen
Discovering boys were more useful than horses
Is part of a motorway pillar.
The river is full of itself: we called it
Every name under the sun.
The order is a guide but not a help.
It will not say what you might say,
Life imitates the art we cannot make.

William Ryan's Song in July

Summer for me has always been August, no other.
I shall travel to no island
For Ryan is not to be fooled. Give me August
Or nothing. Can you understand?

Some fools that I have known have laughed
And cared to demonstrate
That August is the end and not the middle.
Yes, says I, for I chose in that knowledge.

The heat is blackened, full of dust then, Ryan
—I could have told you that.
The trees of an awful non-fighting weight
—Which is lost in a week. I had heard of all that.

August, let me say, is situate
Between July
And sonorous September. It's a sort of middle
For the scary, no place to be in. *Have you heard?*

I shall give you July, for a gift.

The Wild Ass Is Skint

. . . For entertaining you, Madame,
Has consumed my entire allowance.
Hence my dead coat, my one shoe.
And this is why we walk a lot,
Or did. So take the bloody bus again
And meet a better class of death
Than I, whose personal effect
Consists of a spraycan of paint
With which I write these final thoughts.
I am up here with God
And the weak-bladdered gulls
At the top of the world's
Longest single-span suspension bridge,
And you go nicely in between
The praise of Denis Law
And a cunt that might be a Matisse.

You simply drove me up the wall:
Therefore I shall jump in the Humber.
There are no ironies at all,
And here is her telephone number.

In the Head

I watched her coming through the park
And wanted that black hair, that shape,
That curved voice calling me my name,
And as I wanted this I saw
Her life could not be touched by mine.
I know that she is real somewhere,
Her set of rooms and obligations
Owned impossibly without
Me coming up in dreams or talk,
Her earrings, postcards, clothes and love
Invisibly acquired and lost
With birth-certificates and keys:
A life imperial in scale
If I alone could enter it
To map its rich confusion and desire.
You could not count the theories
Aroused and then discredited
In this place in an afternoon,
The shadow pastorals performed
Inside the mind as summer throws
The switch on brick and grass and skin,
And no one minds or needs attend
This conference, and no one dares.
The earth could not support the weight
And raw perfection of despair.

Jazz

It is to you, my dear, I owe
This love of the soloing saxophone.
You are going away, for a while.
I have borne that before.
I am only afraid
Of the highly-strung bass
Like a clock in the groin.

For Lowell George

What fills the heart is felt to make amends,
Until the flooded heart can no more choose
Release than never sing its staggered blues.
I wish you had not found such special friends.
At thirty-four, at three a.m., in bed,
Of overweight helped on by dope and booze,
Before your talent bored you you were dead.

The Beat Goes On
(for Jerry Kidd and John Rowley)

The radio's remembering
Piano-shifting brutalists
In suits of whorish pink, who vocalise
Bluenote-bayous of razz and grief; remembering
Mulatto chords and Mama Roux,
The currency and then the price
The stovepipe-hatted obeah man exacts
For stealing shellac masters
From the tombs of Creole Pharaohs
Still cool in their coke-filled sarcophagi
Under the boardwalks of Hell; remembering
The life we never lived
Again, a riding cymbal-shimmer
Stroked with a hickory Premier C
As the horns stand up in the key of real sex.
Encyclopaedias of air encode
The glamour of the singing poor.
We learn them like a second heart.
They gave the mirror all its moves:
Tonight it will not even laugh –
And for this I have drummed out the grease
From a lifetime of antimacassars,
Nagged by good taste and a future
That looks as high and lonesome now
As a busload of drunks and their delicate axes
Marooned in the snowy Sierras.
There's no cenotaph for those
Who try to cut the cost of touring,
Who go in derailments, in cropdusters' biplanes,
To Klansmen at crossroads,
Shot by their mistreated girls
Or drowned in concrete by the Mob,
And they cannot now honour their contract
To make us a language of passion and style.
But this evening the Sixties,
This evening the King,
So bored he even broadcasts hymns
To the wives of Nebraska and Kansas,

Who sweat at the prospect of leisure
And choke on their sociables, feeling Him move
In the air over wheatfields and highways.
The King keeps his class in the bathroom
With the whips and methadone.
He turns the Baptist Gospel off
And hears the princes practise down the hall.
They are harder and blacker and closer to jail
And the heartbreaking four forty-nine.
Tonight the trailer park gets drunk
Beneath a moon of impotence
As someone seminal awakes
At the wheel of a stolen Chevrolet,
To search the airwaves once again
For something that could make him dance,
With whisky freezing on his shirt
And a writ for his skin in his pocket.

The Next Meeting

Tonight's the turn of Mrs Mac
To address the bereaved
At the Spiritualist Church.
Too cold for snow, the punters say,
But nurse their cars around the park.

She will speak of the comforting aether,
Where voices in a loop rehearse
Their sentence to infinity. Outside
It snows a silent alphabet
That vanishes on contact with the ground.

Midsummer's Eve

A blue light is hung in the house
On these nights in the middle of summer,
When dark never comes, then comes at once,
As if this were no time of year
But time for real inside the head.

There is this half-surprise, the hand
Half-visible before the face,
The softened mirror like a door
To the house where the prizes are given
For coming at all, but you don't move.

When the trains are asleep
Between here and the sea, when the one boat
Is rocked on a slick of the moon,
When the last lamp swings off up its track,
You will always be elsewhere,

Sitting it out on the edge of the map
And rehearsing your book of improvements.
The lamp should be meeting a girl about now.
There she is, on the bench, with her face turned away,
As the cold-eyed crew of the M.V. *Moneta*

Play Cheat and look out for a flame on the cliffs.
They are fools. At this moment their man's
In a room full of smoke with the railway police,
Denying it all but with no cigarettes,
Till the heavies arrive; although the girl

Could change it all, were she awake.
But then, who wants an outcome? Who needs it?
You make your offer to the night.
You say you want no recompense.
The night will take you at your word.

Not Sending Cards this Year

Consoled by the dead with their tea-things
In somebody's lodge in the snowed-under forest,
We listen with them as the end of the world
Comes six months late by pigeon post
As the roar of silk thread and a note
On the death of the definite article.

We watch them tune their metres down –
Revise. Revise. Is it enough
To say the end is like the end?
And we admire such
Intensities of indolence
And call them the point of discomfort.

The best to be had is a biro that works
And some milk left for morning.
Let's go out now, to where we live,
The dead harbour, the pub and the station buffet,
North of the Word, where it rains in your face.

The Widower

Most men hire out their lives
To finish off with nights like this,
The blue from which the darkness pours
Upon the knotted apple tree
To simplify the shape of long neglect,

And some of them have stayed in love
A lifetime with intimate strangers,
Discovered a talent for taking a walk
Or for blether begun at the table at noon
And kept through sleep and next day's lack:

But half will meet the end alone
And from a cramped obituary spell out
A name that cannot now be learned
Though it is said like rosaries
And written down the margins of the page.

I've seen my elders pad their gardens
Uselessly and try to read.
Now there is only leisure to exhaust,
And a tree by the builders' default.
It bore no fruit I ever saw.

But let there be one widower
To see one yellow apple wax
Towards its perihelion
And have his solitude precise
And rich until the tree is dark.

Downstairs

What are they discussing now,
The ones who do their time down there,
The ones who tap-dance and are fried?
What can they ever find to add,
Except that it is very late
Or else the bloody clock has died?

Infants

From the school at the end of the road
The children's cries come like an army
Met to celebrate its strength.
It's like a roar from out of Asia,
One that made the empire twitch.
They simply haven't registered
The rings and fillings in the ditch.

The sons and daughters of my friends
Are small enough now to imagine that we
Are necessary to the real, and kin
To the grave blue bear and the love-squashed mouse.
Desire will conscript them. They will say
They need the keys, and mean the house.

Those in Peril

We are drunk, or the whole place is tilted absurdly.
Perhaps we are sinking.
Holed beneath the waterline,
The ship entombs its novelists
Among the boiling cargo-holds,
While up here the ocean slops in
Through the music-room doors
And underwater strings are heard
To serenade Leviathan.
It was unwise, this ship of stone,
But first-class people do not drown,
And as long as our burden of trinkets is answered in heaven
We should not be scared that the captain
Inflated a single-berth raft over dinner
And left without trying the sweet . . .
Besides, the cabaret maintains morale –
'Miss Margot Virago, red hot from Chicago!'
She may find it chilly
Washed up on the iceberg still wearing her whip
And obliged to discover fulfilment
In living off penguins with Wobbly Ken,
The mad cunt who is shouting abuse
At a bored semicircle of ghosts,
While dogfish snap around his ankles
And wish they were sharks. The sharks wear suits
And cruise between the humans smoothly,
Smiling their ravishing multiple smiles
And throwing their darts like harpoons
While their faces make noises like toilets.
Because they remind us of money,
In bumpers of sorrow we sing
Of the coins we have handled and lost
On these *Narrenschiff* nights with the boys . . .
We love these Northern lassitudes,
But can you call it politics? . . .
We had to tie poor Petchy to the mast:
He could not find it for himself.
He thinks the sirens sing to him –
In fact they are a theatre group

46

Rehearsing *The Bloomsbury Lighthouse Review*
To a chorus of brainbending whines,
Which makes each of us privately pray
Not to end up alone
On the radical feminist lifeboat
Whenever the biscuits run out . . .
I have looked at the ocean and think it is deep
And a place where the dictionaries drown,
But I do not believe we are lost.
There is a legend on this ship
That taking down the head he keeps
Displayed above the fruit machine,
At times of need the Polar Bear
Will pass among us with a hat,
And taking the only course open, set sail
For the land of the takeout, that serves after time.

The Seaside Specialist

As every mag along the front reveals
It is the festival of skin,
So if your own is grey or loose
Lie down with a gatefold and wank
In the sock-smelling fug of your choice,
At which only the mirror will look.
Then read of how the Anabaptists,
Choosing to go naked, played
With nuts and berries and their friends
To be as little children; how
These heretics were brought to book
And burnt in the sociable squares.
It will look like a posture
Supportable only in summer,
Like those embarrassed couples racked
On postcards in primary colours
Of nuptial malfeasance and loathing,
Sent to prove a holiday was had.
Extended families of pain,
They float in batches to the shore
You reach beyond your book at night.
The sea, the blue comedian
Who rolls the drowned along the aisles
Of an interminable act,
Has autographed each card with love.

Gun Law

I wrote a cheque out in the snow
For money in its element.
More white than I was happy with
And cold enough to weld my hand
To the seat of the bike I had bent.

They did not love me at the bank,
Nor would they give me money.
Then I wished I really had
A murder in my heart,
A Gladstone pocket
Equipped for spectacular slayings.
Hey sucker.
Suck on this. Boom-boom.

The crippled bike bore me away
Down drifted tenfoots, over drains,
Around imaginary housing schemes
Into the sleeping sickness of the archives.
With everything in black and white
I am simply awaiting the dogs.

In the tabloids that I dreamed,
I saw the murdered teller rise
Like an overdraft, wearing a smile
Of such inane complacency
It nearly matched his Christmas shirt
And made me want to cry.
He wiped his lips and offered me
His blinding handkerchief.

Out here in limbo in the snow
In a tanner's yard in Wilmington
At dawn I clear the midnight's drift
From stacks of frozen currency.
A wad of burning Zloties heats
My pan of ice, and here, at least,
Though I lie in the arms of the dollar,
The coins on my eyes are my own.

Heatwave

The chestnuts take their shadows in
Like women bearing winding-sheets.
I hear, though I'm not listening,
The night's held breath of fruit and meat,
And all around my skin I feel
The long day's thick residual heat,
Erotic, inescapable.
Someone is dying on our street.

Late

In the rented rooms above the bay
The simmer of epistles was like sleep.
Old men grow bored with young men's books,
But still they followed and were sold
At the stall that an uncle had kept.
His landlady found roses in the hall
Without a note, and for the afternoon
There was the itch of Sundays at the Spa:
Band-music, marble, heat and wickedness.
He did not have to work, she thought.
Eat greens for the conduct; wear sensible shoes;
Keep up with the journal; walk out to the light
At the pier's end, a mile in the ocean.
Look back for the window seen only from here.
It is only a place you can see.
It survives you. It makes you a ghost,
Where she lived, where we both lived once.
I am embarrassed to have stayed
So long and on so little and for this.

Quiet Wedding

This isn't the way to the airport.
No, this is the way
To the backlots of our family romance.
We are sure of a lavish reception,
Warm black wine in every cup,

In the loved setting
Of sofas and grey, guilty light
That their years in the business of hoofing and hating
Have made them the mistresses of.
Miss Crawford, Miss Davis. Miss Davis, Miss Crawford.

The Ring

The autumn stands its light to cool and smoke
On the green tiles, in the bare brown grate.

Through the door, in the park,
The children wrestle in their leafy pit.

It is for them you wager, privately; for them.
You've had your turn. Now hold the ring.

The Lamp

Slowly, these evenings, it warms to its business,
Adding its ivory miniature wattage
To headaches unbidden or begged for;
To love doing overtime, vicious or civil.
A simple but brilliant composure
Of levers and springs, with a bulb and a flex,
It should be an eye but is not, and should know
But does not, and should feel but cannot.
It squats at my shoulder and silently stares,
Giving nothing away of the dreams it can't have.
These dreams concern high cold
And long views from a clinic to Europe
Set out beneath its haze of sun
And politics. No loneliness, no cry,
Can climb to the terrace where money is dying,
In rarefied purple, with desperate good humour.
The lamp is in place by the notes on the desk
In the room that is kept at the dry heat of health
And has four walls of medical journals.
Nobody lives here and no one is missing.
Strange if when some modernist made this
He failed to see its perfect sex. Plug in, turn on
And leave alone: blank ecstasy
Unbounded by the mortal physics.
An anglepoise lamp done in white.
If you were to ask me that now I should act
In reasonable faith to find a name
For what it does, then I would have to say,
You asking me, you being you, and reason being
What it is, and the lamp being here,
A prosthetic of dark in the room,
It sheds light, I suppose. *It depends what you mean.*

Tides
(for Peter Didsbury)

There are tides in the paper that lies on the desk.
They are slow. They are burdened with junk,
The circular diaspora
Of piracy and empires, on the Middle Sea.
They are bored with the half-life of scholarly myth,
Bored with the gaze of the sunblind student
Attacked by nausea on a bus to the Gut,
Where adventure appears in a glass of anis
As a species of maritime fraud
At which the police can only smile
As they sit by the fountain comparing their guns.
There are tides in the inky compartments
Of every such homecoming briefcase,
Tides on every desk. They are waiting
For fools to afflict with the notion of time
As a pool of salt in a frame of sand,
To afflict with the index of names
And the index of those without names,
Which is bigger and harder to freight,
And will turn in its leather-and-brass-bound sleep
And despatch the most scrupulous craft to the bed
On the calmest evening, miles from nowhere,
In waters turned milky by moonlight,
That riffle like ream upon ream of octavo
Spread over the floor and left blank.
The boat is rigged. Someone ships out
Across a sea that never breaks,
Whose storms are always submarine,
Where sinking leaves no watermark.

The Last Japanese Poet in the West

I sit in my emplacement by the Styx,
Disarmed, distracted and alone.

In my cup the ocean scours
The black sands of posterity.

Now nothing, I read, will be moving,
Not even the promising termite.

Now not even lies can be mustered
To restock the atlas of chances

Our nervous historians bought
But could not get on with:

Now not even I am a fool.
For who, when today I emerge

With my briefcase of outmoded hearsay,
My ulcer and Pentel, and step

Into the glare of privacy,
Will greet me with that name?

Bound for Glory

Balanced like an angel band
On the point of the needle, they worship
A polytheistic pharmacopoeia
Where Kali, Manson,
Marx and Kubla Khan give laws,
While the Christ of the Andes dispenses
Cocaine from an old silver box
That someone's girlfriend stole in Leeds.

Oh, the pale expensive
Calm of the culture of drugs
On a Sunday up Holderness Road
When the *Cedar of Lebanon* docks and disgorges
Its rumoured farrago of gold,
When they raise up the takeout
In praise of a talent for passive consumption
Unmatched in the civilized world,
When no man lacks a banker's bag
To scare him in his underpants.

Victims

Some of them like zealots seek
Asylum in the dictionary
And hope that they will not be missed.

Others surrender in public.
They ask a quick death
At the hands, on the tongues,
Of indifferent captors.

Both want to be rid of the future.
There is no escape. They will finish up
Strapped to the big wheel of syntax,
Their names being taken
In vain by the ignorant gods.

Sitting in the Draught

Old age. It's an exile from places
No one now believes were there,
From homelands long abolished and redrawn.
The smells and streetnames that were me
Don't figure in the standard works.
They treat us like expensive cups –
They keep us but the handles break –
Half tenderly and half with young contempt
For what they cannot understand or be.
When I unlock the door I find
A chamber full of fog, where young men smile.
They want me to capitulate
To corridors where madmen weep and piss
Behind the furniture, accompanied
By songs the pianist can't play, with words
No one remembers properly.
I too had parents once. I visited
The lounge where they departed from a world
That could not recognize their lives.
I do not need your compliments
If I am able, still, to offer tea, still less
The number of my books to be remarked
As if I were five and precocious. Now
I need this room to be alone,
To keep the silence company and wait.

From the Narrator's Tale

Whether it happens upstairs or on Pluto
You hear it, but not what it means.
It's the art of narration. You notice
A singular absence of motive.
The pace is a killer. The names are absurd.
A storm of clues among the stars
Comes adrift of its questions
And moves among us now like facts
We can't buy or dispose of. Clear?
A model must be bigger than its source
And most of it be out of sight,
Like Africa from here. Yes, Africa,
Where Hagenbach attempts to con a sheikh.
The world's long curve! Here comes the prose
On paper wings, our Omens of the day.
We hear him fried in Essoline
Before admiring crowds. They love
Their country and the testy Will of Allah.
So tell me, how long is it now
Since Haggers embezzled the Junior Pie?
Of course we always wished him harm –
We did it for the future's sake –
But if that shit can own a soul
That smoulders afterwards, then what,
I ask you, will be made
Of those who really matter here
In this too-long-neglected, imperfectly rendered
Chunk of the whole inadvisable project?
    I sit in the greenhouse and watch
The tomatoes expanding like suns.
Along the heating pipes I hear
The couples and their marriages,
So bored they have even turned back
To the partners with whom they began
For punishment and company. All afternoon
The rows elaborate themselves,
Deranged bureaucracies of noise,
A dire choral symphony
I shall not find the time to write,

Whose theme is custody of pain.
Midsummer's Eve. Tonight's the night.
The template of authority
Is matched against the air. The heat
Rests its gun in the shade of a wall.
And I, as ever, come too soon,
For how else could I tell you these things?

　　Now Endean hangs the paper lamps
Around the arboretum, sullenly
Dreaming a drink to his hand.
His boy rakes leaves across the pool
And by a gift of physics finds
Jane's beckoning reflection there.
Her tongue upon her lips welds his
To the cleft in his palate. His mother
Goes down to the cellar with Simpson.
The vol-au-vents wink into flame.
The cat lies more immobile by the range
As ash flakes down upon its fur.

　　I am tired of telling this prickteasing truth
That I cannot invent or abolish.
How much we resemble the humans we read of.
Attending the party that calls us to meaning,
Finite but unbounded fools
With all our permutations done,
Interred by accident of birth
Among the blazing nebulae,
We'll crowd the balustrade, and looking down
We'll see us dancing, looking up.

Two Finger Exercise

I play my last arpeggio,
Then shut the dummy keyboard and sit back
To listen as the note decays.

It takes its time. It takes mine too.
It's numbering the rûches on the gowns
Of all the roses on this hill

Where England sprays her armpit
With a subtle distillation
Of hypocrisy and bullshit.

The keys are worn with locking nature
In the inventory of air. Let us be human,
Say critics who need a new interest.

They live somewhere else, counting coal
In the virtuous baths of the North
To build a thesis lumpy with endeavour.

This is where the English live.
And we are foreigners. The bus to work
Braves Congos of complacent tat . . .

The evenings, though, are "personal".
I count the rooms. I count again.
I try to sit in one of them. I fail

And imagine pianos instead,
A Bechstein warehouse, grand and dumb,
With teeth as white as privilege.

The Captain's Pipe

Before the poor are working I am here,
Before the air is used or the first kiss planted
Or the heat of Kundalini blooms
At the base of the initiate spines.
I dislike the cities, the plains
And this olive drab sweatbox,
The jungle, in one of whose inlets
I anchor and watch without interest or boredom
Green ocean contending with dun yellow river
For rights to the seasnakes, the Lascar morsels.
Left to me, self-interest looks like fate.
Tending the bowl with a fragrant brown thumb
I denature the Buddha: look
How he diversifies in smoke.
A million tawdry gods appear –
Damp earth and bamboo, stuck with feathers,
False dawn's birds of paradise.
Let them declare
That man too is commerce,
Like opals and copra, like gold.
Let exiled bureaucrats
Have cold clear dreams of this
As they twist on starched beds
In the nervous cantonment,
A mile from my imminent pleasure.
Happy the man with a pipe to his name
As the sun steps smoking from the sea
Like a worthy untainted by trade.
On his breast he displays
The gold disc of exemption,
From which all the money was anciently copied,
According to one of the poets I hanged.
I take a lens and polish it,
The first rays warm to the map at my feet.
The first cannon cracks, the citadel chars,
And by evening the gold in its cellars
Will melt like the sun in the water.

The Amateur God

Like sluggish electrons
The first gnats of April
Are cruising the visual field.
The kingfisher's moulting its plaster of Paris.
The cherub is moulting his head.
The goldfish stare up from cushions of weed,
Rehearsing blasé vowels at the sun.
The Peace Rose,
Pruned to a barbed wire paradox,
Stands with its label, as if on a platform
Awaiting the slow train of summer.
The gardener beats a new path out of cinder.
The brazier rolls its crimson eyes
Like Argus. There's nothing but detail
And leisure to name it, with one hand
To cool in the pond, and the other
Rubbing moss into my jeans
Wholeheartedly at thirty as at three.
The afternoon is permanent.
My father, my uncle, in suits of pale ash,
Are still sinking the black in the shade.
The voices of their politics
Are softer than the fountain's voice.
The afternoon is permanent.
The amateur god of this garden is me.